Y0-BRD-179

The BEATLES

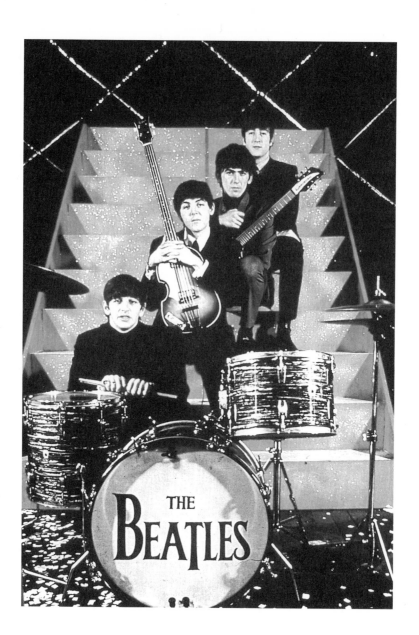

Biography

The **BEATLES**

Jeremy Roberts

A&E

Lerner Publications Company
Minneapolis

For Bobby—yeah, yeah, yeah . . .

A&E and **BIOGRAPHY** are trademarks of the A&E Television Networks, registered in the United States and other countries.

Some of the people profiled in this series have also been featured in A&E's acclaimed BIOGRAPHY series, which is available on videocassette from A&E Home Video. Call 1-800-423-1212 to order.

Copyright © 2002 by Jim DeFelice

All rights reserved. International copyright secured. No part of this book may be reproduced, stored in a retrieval system, or transmitted in any form or by any means—electronic, mechanical, photocopying, recording, or otherwise—without the prior written permission of Lerner Publications Company, except for the inclusion of brief quotations in an acknowledged review.

This book is available in two editions:
Library binding by Lerner Publications Company,
    a division of Lerner Publishing Group
Softcover by First Avenue Editions,
    an imprint of Lerner Publishing Group
241 First Avenue North
Minneapolis, MN 55401 U.S.A.

Website address: www.lernerbooks.com

Library of Congress Cataloging-in-Publication Data

Roberts, Jeremy, 1956–
    The Beatles / by Jeremy Roberts.
       p.   cm. — (A&E biography)
    Includes discography, filmography, bibliographical references, and index.
    ISBN: 0–8225–4998–0 (lib.bdg. : alk. paper)
    ISBN: 0–8225–5002–4 (pbk. : alk. paper)
    1. Beatles—Juvenile literature. 2. Rock musicians—England—Biography—Juvenile literature. I. Title. II. Biography (Lerner Publications Company)
ML3930.B39 R63 2002
782.42166'092'2—dc21   00–012935

Manufactured in the United States of America
1 2 3 4 5 6 – JR – 07 06 05 04 03 02

CONTENTS

John Lennon, age fifteen, and the Quarry Men at their first gig in 1955

PROLOGUE:
FIRST ENCOUNTERS

The two boys eyed each other. John had just finished playing with his band at a church festival in Liverpool, England. With his hair slicked back and pants pegged tight, he looked like a tough—a "teddy boy" as the look was called. Not yet seventeen, he was the guitarist and leader of a band called the Quarry Men.

Paul briefly glanced at John. He'd dressed up for the festival, trying to impress some girls. Now he found himself trying to impress the band members instead. Someone handed him a guitar. He fingered the strings and cranked into "Twenty Flight Rock," an early hit by American rock 'n' roller Eddie Cochran.

John was impressed, though he barely nodded. Paul followed up with another pop song, then a medley of hits by Little Richard, another American rock musician. Somewhere along the way, Paul played "Long Tall Sally," a Little Richard song he was always working on.

And that was that. The Quarry Men played another set. Paul turned his attention back to what he'd come to do— pick up girls. He drifted toward the edge of the crowd as the group played, then moved on to the local pub.

But this chance meeting in 1957 would change the history of pop music. For the two young men who'd met in the steaming hot church hall were John Lennon and Paul McCartney. Together, they would become one of music's greatest creative teams. Along with George Harrison and Ringo Starr, they would form The Beatles, the most important rock group ever.

The Beatles' arrival in Toronto in 1964 caused Canadian fans of all ages to shriek with excitement.

Their songs would be played across the world. People would scream and faint when they performed.

While it would take several difficult years of hard work and disappointment, once The Beatles made it, they *really* made it. They helped define the music we call rock 'n' roll. They also helped define the 1960s. The sixties were a time of youthful change and creativity—a time of "Revolution," to borrow one of The Beatles' song titles. The Beatles were a major part of that revolution.

The Beatles performed in an era of rapid changes in technology as well as music. Their images were sent by television and radio across the world. For a while many considered them as famous as God. But the reality of The Beatles was always much larger than the image generated by and for the media. Their talents were such that nothing could contain them, not even hysteria and hype so crazy it was called Beatlemania. Ironically, that talent—and maybe the sixties themselves—doomed the group in the end.

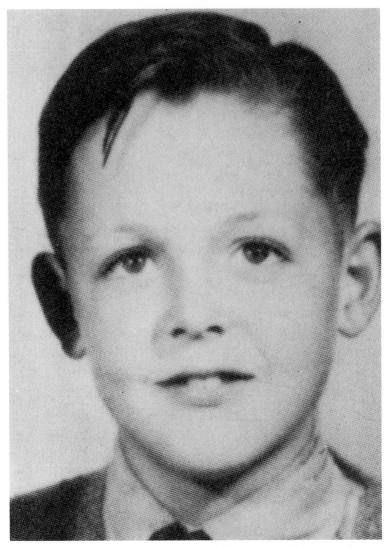

Paul McCartney was born and raised in Liverpool, England, where he later helped form The Beatles.

Chapter **ONE**

"A TASTE OF HONEY"

EXCEPT FOR THEIR GUITARS, JOHN LENNON AND Paul McCartney didn't seem to have much in common when they met that hot summer day in Liverpool. For one thing, John was almost two years older than Paul. He was born on October 9, 1940. Paul was born on June 18, 1942. John's family was middle class. Paul's was working class. In England at the time, these differences could mean a lot. Some people would not associate with members of a different class.

There were other differences as well. In school, Paul was a more attentive student. John would cut class and toss erasers, getting in trouble. By modern standards, these antics don't seem very bad. At the time, however, they were serious enough to label John a troublemaker.

On the other hand, the boys had some important things in common. Both had gone through difficult family trials. Paul's mother died a few months before the pair met. John's father abandoned John and his mother soon after John was born. Though his mother lived nearby, John was raised by his mother's sister and her husband, Mimi and George Smith. George, who was very close to John, died when John was thirteen.

Both boys grew up in families and a city that had seen better days. Located at the mouth of the Mersey River in northwestern England, Liverpool had many factories as well as an important seaport. The Germans had bombed much of the city during World War II. It was rebuilt after the war, but changes in the British and world economy made Liverpool less important than it had once been. By the 1950s, many of its industries were struggling or had moved away. The city's many working-class people often had a hard time finding jobs and paying for necessities.

Still, Liverpool was an important port for ships traveling to and from the United States. Americans often came to the city, bringing with them American goods, American music, and American ideas. Because it was an industrial city as well as a seaport, Liverpool had a reputation as a tough place, much as American cities such as Pittsburgh and Detroit do. Both the American influence and the tough-guy image would be important to Lennon and McCartney as they honed their musical skills.

The fact that Liverpool was relatively far from London also played a role in Lennon and McCartney's future. At the time, the important English recording companies were located in London. Many people there looked down on musical groups from outside the city, especially those from working-class towns like Liverpool. This attitude presented one more barrier for the young musicians to overcome.

The most important things John Lennon and Paul McCartney had in common were their creativity and intelligence. Once they met, they egged each other on to improve their musical skills and learn more. Something sparked in that hot church hall in 1957. It quickly grew into a raging inferno. "That was the day," Lennon later said, "the day I met Paul, that it started moving."

A few days later, Lennon had a friend ask McCartney if he'd care to join the Quarry Men.

SKIFFLE

The Quarry Men were named after Quarry Bank School, the school the original members attended. The band played skiffle, a cross between American bluegrass, country, rhythm and blues, and early rock 'n' roll music. An English style, skiffle had a primitive sound that featured banjos and a washboard. Washboards were used to clean clothes in the days before families had home washing machines. Rubbing a hard object across the surface of a washboard produced a shuffling kind of percussion sound.

The teenage Quarry Men weren't very good at first. John Lennon didn't even know how to tune his guitar when Paul met him. But they were willing to learn, and they put in long hours practicing and listening to rock 'n' roll music. Learning was an adventure. One day, McCartney and Lennon journeyed by bus across the city to meet a guitarist who could show them how to play B7, a common guitar chord in rock music. Another day, they hunted down someone with a hard-to-find American record.

Most people, including their relatives, didn't think much of music as a career. Paul's father had played piano and trumpet with his own band during the 1920s. But he gave up music for a steady job in the cotton trade, where he worked as a salesman after the war. John's aunt, Mimi Smith, was a strict though loving guardian. She bought him his first guitar, but she wasn't enthusiastic about music. "A guitar's all right," she used to tell him. "But you'll never earn your living by it."

GEORGE, STU, AND THE SILVER BEATLES

As John and Paul got better, so did the Quarry Men. At some point in 1958, Paul convinced John to let another friend, George Harrison, join the group. Born on February 25, 1943, Harrison was the youngest

John Lennon was raised by his aunt Mimi Smith, even though his mother lived nearby.

member of the band, but he was already good enough on the guitar to play lead. His father was a bus driver and union official. His mother, interested in music and dance, did everything she could to encourage her son's interest in the guitar.

The other original members of the Quarry Men soon found other interests and left the band. But John, Paul, and George continued to play together and hone their craft. They also continued to go to school. Paul and George went to high school at the Liverpool Institute. John attended the Liverpool Art College, located next door to the high school.

The trio all played guitars. They added a bass guitar player when John convinced a friend named Stuart Sutcliffe to join them. Stu was a talented artist—he had sold a painting for a large sum of money—but he couldn't play the bass very well. But he was a friend of John's and helped fill out the band's sound as it continued to grow.

Somewhere along the way, the teenagers started calling themselves the Silver Beatles. The origin of the name seems hazy, even to the band members. Recalling their early days, John, Paul, and George usually told writers that the inspiration had come from an American rock group, Buddy Holly and the Crickets. Changing the spelling of the insect name "beetles" to "Beatles" made for a pun on the word *beat,* as early rock 'n' roll was sometimes called.

But Paul told biographer Barry Miles that the name might actually have come from a movie. "We were

The Silver Beatles, George, left, *John,* middle, *and Paul,* right, *standing outside Paul's Liverpool home*

Marlon Brando's portrayal of Johnny in the 1953 film The Wild One *defined the image of a tough rebel.*

into the Marlon Brando film *The Wild One,"* he recalled. "And in that they use the word beetles, and we think that kind of clinched it." At the time, McCartney added, the band thought "the Beetles" were members of Brando's motorcycle gang. But the nickname actually referred to the bikers' girlfriends.

The Silver Beatles played a variety of dance halls and rough clubs in the Liverpool area for little pay. They toured Scotland. They even backed a striptease act. As they struggled, they got better, learning by doing—and doing and doing and doing. Lennon and McCartney began to collaborate on songwriting, but most of the tunes that the Silver Beatles played were covers—songs by other artists.

The important influences on the group were American: Elvis Presley, Buddy Holly, Little Richard, Jerry Lee Lewis, and Chuck Berry, to name a few. Their music had a harder edge and beat than the most popular groups of the time. In Britain, for example, Cliff

Richard and the Shadows emphasized a softer, more melodic approach to rock and pop ballads.

Best on Drums

Still raw, the band slowly gathered fans. They had one serious problem, however—they lacked a steady drummer. Different drummers played with them on occasion, but for many of their gigs in 1959 and 1960, they played without any drums at all. In the summer of 1960, Paul called up Pete Best, a drummer who had played with them at times in the past. Pete's mother owned a small Liverpool club called the Casbah, where the band had played, on and off, since it opened in the summer of 1959.

"Paul said had I still got any drums," Best remembered later. "I told him I'd just got a complete new kit. . . . He said they'd got a job in Hamburg [Germany] and was I interested in being their drummer? . . . I'd get [£15] a week, which was a lot. Much better than going to a training college."

At the time, £15 a week was considered a decent working man's pay. For a teenager who wanted to be a musician, it was a fortune.

"Make Show"

If Liverpool had a reputation for being a tough town, Hamburg's reputation was ten times worse. And the German city lived up—or down—to that reputation. Gunrunning smugglers, gangsters, prostitutes—you

The Silver Beatles, from left to right: *Paul, Pete Best (their original drummer), George, and John*

could find them all in the area of clubs and bars known as the St. Pauli district. Exactly the place for a green and growing rock 'n' roll band to learn its trade. To the Silver Beatles, Hamburg looked like the big time.

During the fall of 1960, the Silver Beatles performed long, grinding sets in the St. Pauli district. They started in a bar called the Indra, known for its violent brawls. According to rock historians Bob Cepican and Ali Waleed, at least one shooting occurred at the Indra while the Silver Beatles performed there. The police soon closed the Indra, and the band moved on to the Kaiserkeller, another bar owned by the same man.

The German audience liked the group's rough sound and their tough-guy act. John would insult the crowd and do crazy things like giving the outlawed Nazi salute. They would joke between sets and interact with the audience. Bruno Koschmider, the club owner, encouraged them to *mach shau*—"make show." Their wild performances were good for business.

Somewhere along the way, the group dropped "Silver" from its name. The German audiences loved to pronounce "Beatles" as *peedles,* which punned into a dirty word. The Beatles didn't mind. "We used to do crazy things because we were identified as the *Verrueckt* Beatles, which was the crazy Beatles," Pete Best said later. "John would split his jeans and there would be mock fights onstage. We'd jump off the stage and dance with the audience and run around

The Beatles donned leather clothes that made them look a bit like outlaws.

and stamp our feet. . . . The faster the music, the faster the German crowd went wild."

But a lot more was going on. The Beatles honed their act. Their music got tighter. They learned how to please people with a combination of humor and attitude that complemented the music. "They suddenly found that there was something different from playing for the rest of their lives in Liverpool," said Billy Harry, who covered the Liverpool music scene in his newspaper, the *Mersey Beat*. "I don't think they thought of big success before that time. . . . They were so excited. They weren't swollen heads; it was enthusiasm."

But their time in Hamburg came to a crashing conclusion in December 1960, when George was deported from Germany because he was underage. Shortly afterward, Paul McCartney and Pete Best were arrested. Police charged that they had started a small fire in the basement of a theater. Details of what happened vary, but Paul and Pete were told to leave Germany. John quickly followed. Stu had become engaged to a local girl named Astrid Kirchner and decided to stay with her.

Rockin' Liverpool

The band had left Liverpool as teenagers trying to figure out how to play music. They came back to England confirmed rock 'n' rollers. Dressed in leather, interspersing humor with their sharp rock 'n' roll, The Beatles had a unique image and sound. The uniqueness quickly became apparent at the Cavern Club, a large, sweltering basement club in downtown Liverpool. They won a standing lunchtime gig there. Within a few weeks they had a dedicated following.

Their song lineup included a number of original compositions written by John and Paul. These tunes caught the energy and vitality of their roaring stage show. The lyrics had a bouncy playfulness that became their trademark. Creatively, the songs were miles ahead of the music the band had performed just a few months before.

The Beatles returned to Hamburg in April 1961 and stayed for thirteen weeks, playing to wildly enthusiastic audiences. While Stuart sat in on some of the performances, at least at the beginning, Paul took over as bass player. He wasn't enthusiastic about it at first. Little did he know that he would become the most famous bass player in rock history.

"I definitely didn't want to do it but Stuart left," said Paul, "and I got lumbered with it." John couldn't play bass, and George played lead guitar, so it was up to Paul to learn.

"Paul was one of the most innovative bass players that ever played bass," said John many years later. "Not technically great," Lennon added. "None of us were technical musicians. None of us could read music. None of us can write it. But as pure musicians, as inspired humans to make noise, [we're] as good as anyone!"

Playing monster sets from 7 P.M. to 2 A.M., The Beatles continued to polish their act in Germany. They appeared for a while with Tony Sheridan, a well-known British guitarist and singer. With Sheridan, they recorded a few songs, including a rock version of "My Bonnie Lies over the Ocean," a popular song written in 1881.

Generally, the group lined up with George on lead guitar, John on rhythm guitar, and Paul on bass. John and Paul alternated lead vocals. Their music combined the "hard" style of performers like Chuck Berry with pleasing melodies and prominent harmonies—the blending of different voices. While they wrote some of their own songs, The Beatles played a wide range of covers. Their versatility would be a trademark for the rest of their careers.

Back in Liverpool at the beginning of July, The Beatles played the Cavern and similar clubs. That fall, John and Paul took a brief vacation to Paris. When they returned, they were wearing their hair brushed forward with a straight trim, a cut sometimes called "the French style."

It would soon become known as "The Beatles style."

Brian Epstein's persistence and belief in the group were indispensable to The Beatles' success.

Chapter **TWO**

"PLEASE PLEASE ME"

NEATLY DRESSED IN A WELL-TAILORED SUIT, BRIAN Epstein descended the steps to a dank, dark cellar full of noise. The businessman clutched his briefcase handle firmly. He was shy by nature, and this was not the kind of place he went to often. The Liverpool bar was filled with rowdy rock 'n' roll fans. Most of them were much younger than he was. Many were decidedly not the kind of people his well-to-do family associated with.

But Epstein had a mission this late fall day in 1961. He was going to sell himself to the four leather-clad musicians on the Cavern stage. Brian Epstein, who ran the record division of his family's department store, had come to ask The Beatles if he could be their manager.

Epstein had to fight his way to the stage. Finally, he reached George Harrison. He shook hands and said he wanted to discuss something after the show. Maybe he could help the group, he added, not explaining how.

Harrison took the message to the others. Later in the day, they showed up in the department store. "Quite simply, you need a manager," Epstein told them after he led them past the displays of appliances. "Would you like me to do it?"

They said yes.

"Eppy"

Born September 19, 1934, Brian Epstein was the oldest son of a well-known Jewish family in Liverpool. While he had studied for a while to be an actor, Epstein clearly had a talent for business management. He took over the record division of his family's store in late 1957. He did so well that record sales became the most profitable part of the business. Brian was a serious fan of classical music, but he also wrote a column on rock 'n' roll for the *Mersey Beat*.

The majority of Liverpool's residents were Christians, so his religion made Brian different. But he was also different because he was homosexual, or gay. In the 1960s, gay people faced heavy discrimination. The Beatles knew Epstein was gay and occasionally made fun of him. But they also respected him and valued him tremendously as a manager, and in some ways as a father figure.

Epstein had never managed a musical group before. His inexperience would lead him to make mistakes. On the other hand, he was intelligent and creative. He was able to oversee and coordinate many details to get a job done. He had a knack for figuring out what people wanted, and he was a good salesman. He also had complete and total faith in The Beatles.

Epstein had two short-range goals. The first was to increase the amount of money The Beatles received for shows. This he did by finding new places for them to play. His second goal was to get them a record contract with a major company. Without records, The Beatles' music would never reach a large audience. Nor would they make much money.

Because Epstein ran a successful record store, he knew many people in the music industry. But most of these people were salesmen. The people who made records worked in different divisions. They were difficult to reach, let alone persuade. Still, Epstein was able to use his contacts to get a few record company scouts to listen to The Beatles. Most didn't think The Beatles had what it took to succeed. After they recorded demos in January 1962, Epstein met with representatives of Decca, a large record company that distributed Elvis Presley's records in England. "Not to mince words, Mr. Epstein, we don't like your boys' sound," said one of the officials. "Groups are out; four-piece groups with guitars particularly are finished."

"You must be out of your mind," Epstein responded. "You get these boys on TV and you will have an explosion. I am completely confident that one day they will be bigger than Elvis Presley."

Epstein knew that the hard-core rebel look wasn't popular with audiences outside Liverpool—or with the record companies. So he convinced The Beatles to wear specially tailored mohair suits with narrow lapels. Although the suits clashed with The Beatles'

The Beatles gave up their tough-guy look for what would later become their trademark mohair suits.

George Martin, record producer, wasn't immediately impressed with The Beatles but eventually gave them their big chance.

rough image and rebellious personalities, the band members agreed to wear them. They also tightened their stage act.

Perseverance

Neither the cleaner look nor better demos (recordings made to help sell the band to record producers) convinced anyone to sign the group. But Epstein kept at it. Finally that May, he contacted George Martin, a producer at a record label called Parlophone. Though Parlophone's parent company, EMI, had turned down The Beatles, Martin hadn't been involved in that decision. He agreed to have The Beatles audition for him.

At this time, The Beatles were in Hamburg for a series of shows there. When they arrived, they learned that their friend and former band mate, Stu Sutcliffe, had died. He'd had a brain hemorrhage, perhaps as a result of injuries from a fight after a show more than a year earlier. The band members were shocked and saddened, but the news of the audition lifted their spirits. John and Paul wrote a song called "Love Me Do" to play at the audition.

Martin didn't seem impressed when they played. He would "let them know," he said. The Beatles had heard that before. More than a month later, however, Martin told Brian Epstein that he'd like to take a chance on the group. At the time, CDs and cassette tapes hadn't been invented. Instead people listened to records, hard vinyl disks that were played on a turntable. Long-playing records, called LPs or albums, held five to eight songs per side. Short records, called singles or 45s, held one song per side. New groups usually put out a single or two first. If people liked the singles, the group would then make a full album. Martin offered to record and release a single for The Beatles.

Financially, the offer wasn't very good. The Beatles would earn an English farthing, or one-quarter penny, for each record they sold. Still, the opportunity was great news to Epstein and The Beatles. There was one condition, however: They'd have to have a different drummer record with them in the studio. Pete Best wasn't good enough.

"PETE FOREVER, RINGO NEVER"

John, Paul, and George had had doubts about Pete Best for some time. When Brian Epstein told them that George Martin wanted to bring in a new drummer, the band members came to their own decision—Pete was out. In his place, they wanted a drummer named Richard Starkey, known as Ringo Starr. And they wanted Brian to break the news to Pete.

Brian did, the morning after a show—and before Pete knew that the group had been offered a recording contract. He was shocked. So were the fans. Girls

Ringo Starr had more than one offer to perform with another band but decided to join the up-and-coming Beatles.

camped out in front of Best's home. Banners all over Liverpool proclaimed "Pete forever, Ringo Never," but they did no good.

Ringo Starr began drumming in 1956, at age sixteen, as part of a band called the Eddie Clayton Skiffle Group. Around 1959 he joined Rory Storm and the Raving Texans, later known as the Hurricanes. Until 1961 they were better known—and better paid—than The Beatles.

Ringo had a good sense of humor, experience playing to big crowds and he was a decent rock drummer. He also had a great deal of stamina, important for live performances. He could carry the beat through a long, grinding gig. According to Philip Norman, who wrote the book *Shout!*, Ringo's band mates in the Hurricanes called him Rings and then Ringo because he wore so many rings. Starkey was changed to Starr, adds Norman, so that the Hurricanes could bill his drum solo as "Starr Time."

Rory Storm and the Hurricanes had played in Hamburg in 1961. He even played with The Beatles occasionally. So it was natural for them to turn to him when they kicked out Pete Best in August 1962. Ringo didn't know that the group was about to make music history. His decision to join them was purely practical. "I got another offer at the same time, from King Size Taylor and the Dominoes," Ringo said some years later. "He offered twenty pounds a week. The Beatles offered twenty-five, so I took them."

John Lennon first met Cynthia Powell, left, *later his wife, while at school in Liverpool, England.*

A HIT

The Beatles' years of hard work were starting to pay off in a big way. At the same time, John Lennon's relationship with his girlfriend, Cynthia Powell, took its own turn: Cynthia told him she was pregnant. "Don't worry, Cyn," he told her when he found out. "We'll get married."

Lennon's Aunt Mimi had a screaming fit when he told her about the situation. But she eventually gave him the money for a gold wedding ring. With help from Brian Epstein and with Paul McCartney as a witness, the pair were married on August 23, 1962. (Their son, Julian, was born on April 8, 1963.) While John's marriage wasn't a secret, it wasn't publicized either. Epstein knew that an important part of The

WRITING THE SONGS

ohn Lennon and Paul McCartney wrote most of The Beatles' songs, including nearly every song that is considered a classic. From the very beginning to the very end of the band's existence, their songs were authored as "Lennon/McCartney."

But while the credit was always the same, not every song was written the same way. Some were true collaborations, which Paul and John worked out together. Others were composed mostly by just Paul or John, with the other one helping to fill out the music or words later on. Although the two songwriters often had different approaches, they were somehow able to make their songs harmonious.

John's songs had a harder edge; his attitude could be bitter or even angry. His lyrics often came from his personal experiences. Paul's music tended to be more melodic and pleasing to the ear. His songs generally had a musical hook—a catchy sound or chorus. Both songwriters learned from one another and criticized and helped improve each other's work. "My contribution to Paul's songs was always to add a little bluesy edge to them. . . . He provided a lightness, an optimism, while I would always go for the sadness, the discords, the bluesy notes," said John.

"One of the best things about Lennon and McCartney," Paul told an interviewer, "was the competitive element within the team. It was great. I could do stuff he might not be in the mood for, egg him in a certain direction he might not want to go in. And he could do the same for me."

"Had John never met Paul, and vice versa, I firmly believe that neither of them would have turned out to be the great songwriters that they were," added producer George Martin. "They would have been good, but not blisteringly great, as millions of us think they are. Each had a tremendous influence on the other, which neither of them consciously realized."

Beatles' image, specifically for female fans, was sex appeal. Married men didn't sell.

The first Beatles single, "Love Me Do," was released soon after the marriage, on October 5, 1962. "The first time I heard 'Love Me Do' on the radio, I went shivery all over," recalled George Harrison. He'd stayed up all night to hear the record broadcast on Radio Luxembourg, a popular outlet for new pop songs at the time. The record received decent airtime on the radio and did well on the charts, the rankings of pop record sales. It moved slowly to the number seventeen spot—good for a new group. "I didn't think [the song] was all that brilliant, but I was very thrilled by the reaction to The Beatles and their sound," recalled George Martin. "The problem now was to get a follow-up record for them."

Martin suggested a song written by someone else, but The Beatles didn't like it. They wanted to record their own songs. This idea was somewhat unusual at the time. Most groups used music from different writers, always searching for a hit. Martin challenged the band to come up with a song as good as the one he suggested. So Lennon and McCartney went to work. On November 26, 1962, they came back from an engagement in Hamburg to record "Please Please Me."

The record was released in January 1963. Within a few weeks, it was the country's number-one pop song. The Beatles had become the hottest band in Great Britain.

Police became necessary to control crowds as Beatlemania spread. Barriers keep fans back at London's airport.

Chapter **THREE**

BEATLEMANIA

DESCRIBING A TORNADO IS EASY—IF YOU'RE A FEW miles away. If you're in the middle of the storm, though, it's hard to say exactly what's going on. You pitch and whirl, carried around by the wind. You have no control. The best you can do is go along for the ride.

The Beatles were caught up in a tornado in 1963. They didn't know it at first. When they realized what was happening, all they could do was hold on for the ride.

Their talent and hard work helped make it all possible. But other forces were also at work. No one could have predicted the wild craziness that seemed to consume all of England in 1963. Suddenly, everyone *had* to have a Beatles album. Suddenly, everyone *had* to hear them. And see them. And touch them.

A Beatles Storm

The single "Please Please Me" marched to the top of the sales charts in February 1963. On February 11, the group hunkered down in EMI's London studios to record a full album. From roughly 10 A.M. to 11 P.M., with only a few short breaks, they laid down the tracks for a fourteen-song LP. "What I tried to do was to create the live pop group on tape," said Norman Smith, the recording engineer. "I tried to get the sound of The Beatles singing and playing as they'd perform onstage. I thought if I didn't do it, I'd lose the excitement."

The last song in the session—and the last song on the album—was "Twist and Shout," popularized by the Isley Brothers, an African-American group regarded as rhythm and blues pioneers. The Beatles had often used the song to end their shows at the Cavern. "John absolutely screamed it," said George Martin. "God knows what it did to his larynx because it made a sound like tearing flesh." Lennon's screams combined with the rising vocal harmonies and the song's driving beat. While the band may have been tired by the time the session was over, the raw energy of their live shows still came through.

Released on March 22, 1963, the album, also called *Please Please Me*, shot to number one on the charts and stayed there for thirty weeks. Besides the title song, other works included "I Saw Her Standing There," "Love Me Do," and "Do You Want to Know a

Secret." All were destined to become Beatles anthems.

Before and after the album came out, The Beatles played a grueling schedule of live performances. Sometimes they played two concerts in the same day. They performed on a series of radio shows. They made many television appearances. They often raced from an interview to a show, traveling more than one hundred miles in a few hours. In July they began recording a new album, *With the Beatles,* which was released in November. Before it came out, record stores ordered three hundred thousand copies—a huge advance order in Great Britain. But even that amount wasn't enough as the record soared up the charts.

The media only added to the band's popularity. Live performances on radio brought their music to mass audiences. In the newspapers, story after story kept them in front of the public. Writers gave them clever nicknames, such as "The Fab Four." Another nickname, "lovable mop tops," referred to the band members' haircuts. At a time when most men and boys wore crew cuts or other close-cropped styles, The Beatles' hair was considered quite long and even a little outrageous. The style quickly caught on among their teenage fans.

In October the group appeared on *Sunday Night at the Palladium,* the most popular television show in England at the time. The Beatles played five songs and made themselves well known to the public. Before the show, a large group of teenagers gathered outside,

Two thousand screaming fans saw The Beatles perform on Sunday Night at the Palladium, an English television show.

hoping to see the band. About fifty of them managed to break into the auditorium and surrounded The Beatles during their rehearsal. The media played up the event the next day. One newspaper, the *Daily Mirror,* called the fans' chaos "Beatlemania." The word would soon be used over and over again.

Any doubts about their popularity were banished when they were invited to perform for Queen Elizabeth and other members of the royal family in early November. Known as the Royal Command Performance, the televised show was very important in England. Getting invited was an honor and an opportunity. In the space of four songs, The Beatles won the British royalty as fans. Their appearance also showed how important teenage music—and teens in general—had suddenly become. The invitation to play for the queen meant that The Beatles' music was being taken seriously, not dismissed as something just "for kids." The Beatles and their fans had come of age.

Before beginning the last song, John joked with the audience, asking those "in the cheap seats"—those sitting downstairs—to clap. "Those upstairs, rattle your jewelry," he joked. Lennon's joke got a laugh at the show and was repeated in the newspapers the next day. The remark was a comment on the different classes in England. The rich and aristocratic—including the queen—lived separately from the working class, or commoners. Lennon's joke was called "cheeky"— brash and a little irreverent. But this attitude was part of The Beatles' attraction for young people. The band members seemed like rebels, and many young people were filled with rebellious spirit.

On the other hand, The Beatles could be irreverent without threatening people. They seemed friendly and happy. They were always joking and making fun, especially of themselves. The suits that Brian Epstein insisted they wear helped make them acceptable, as well as instantly recognizable. And their songs were appealing. After all, they were all about love.

The Beatles' hit songs reversed "the tiresome trend towards weepie lost-love wailers," an EMI press release explained. The songs were "happy-go-lucky," continued the press release. A writer for the *Daily Mirror* summed up the group's appeal this way: "You have to be a real sour square not to love the nutty, noisy, happy handsome Beatles."

ACROSS THE OCEAN

By late 1963, The Beatles were the top rock act in Great Britain. They had two number-one albums and drew large crowds wherever they played. Their fame went beyond the music world. Nearly everyone seemed to know who they were, thanks to hundreds and hundreds of news stories about them. Their music was innovative and influential, a British twist on American rock 'n' roll. Music writers even compared John and Paul to Beethoven, ranking them among the greatest composers of all time.

But they were barely known in the United States. It wasn't because they hadn't tried. Four Beatles singles had been released in the United States, but none sold very well. Many people felt that the "English sound" didn't appeal to American ears. Brian Epstein was determined to make The Beatles as big in the United States as they were in England. Because the United States was so much larger than Britain, any band that succeeded there could make a lot of money. And because rock 'n' roll had started in the United States, winning over American fans was the true test for any rock musician.

In November 1963, Brian Epstein arranged for a New York City concert. He also managed to get Capitol Records to agree to release Beatles albums in the

United States. Capitol was a large company and had a better chance than the others for good sales. Most important Epstein struck a deal to get The Beatles on *The Ed Sullivan Show.*

The Ed Sullivan Show, a variety show, was one of the most popular television programs in the United States. All sorts of acts—comedians, dancers, even puppeteers—appeared on the show every Sunday night. The deal Epstein struck with the show was not very good financially. But it guaranteed that The Beatles would be the headline act for two shows, the first in February 1964. That arrangement would give them prestige as well as a big audience.

In early January, to set up their American visit, The Beatles released "I Want to Hold Your Hand" as a single in the United States. The song made the American list of the top one hundred hits, but just barely.

The next week, it hit forty-two.

The third week, it went to number one.

Beatlemania was about to sweep the United States.

ON TOP OF THE WORLD

As they landed in Kennedy Airport in New York, The Beatles looked out the windows of their Pan Am airliner. The terminal building was swarming with fans. The band was used to this sort of crowd in England, but they were surprised to see it in United States, where they'd never before been. They were awed. Inside the terminal, reporters mobbed the group in a mad rush.

About 73 million people watched as Ed Sullivan, center, *introduced The Beatles on American television in 1964.*

The Beatles joked with the reporters, in what would become their typical fashion:

> Reporter: Will you sing for us?
> Beatles: No!
> Reporter: Is it because you can't sing?
> John: We need money first.
> Reporter: Why do you sing like Americans but speak with an English accent?
> John: It sells better.
> Reporter: Are you in favor of lunacy?
> Paul: It's healthy.

Ed Sullivan had his largest audience ever when The Beatles played their first show. Teenagers in the auditorium, especially the girls, screamed all through the act. Those watching at home sat glued to their TV sets. People everywhere talked about the group the next day. American girls tried to decide which Beatle was the cutest. There was a rush on jellybeans, which George had mentioned he liked. Both Ed Sullivan concerts were wildly successful.

"What happened in the States was just like Britain, only ten times bigger," said Ringo. The press coverage, the crowds, the record sales—everything multiplied. And success in the United States meant The Beatles were now an international phenomenon.

WHY?

Other groups and performers, from Frank Sinatra to Elvis Presley, had attracted large, hysterical crowds of teenagers. But The Beatles and Beatlemania seemed to go beyond anything that had happened before. The crowds were larger and stayed longer. The group's impact reached further into society. The craziness was, well, crazier. Why? The answer can't be easily summed up.

Some critics contend that The Beatles came to the United States at a low point for American pop music. There was no one dominant super group at the time. Innovators like Chuck Berry had done their best work years before. Some rockers, such as Jerry Lee Lewis, had earned bad reputations because of personal scandals. Other rock musicians, like Buddy Holly, had died young. The Beatles helped fill a musical void, some critics say, even if no one realized there was a void at the time.

Another important factor was the music itself. Many popular performers of the early 1960s, including Roy Orbison, Sam Cooke, and Frankie Valli and the Four Seasons, were known for slow and sad love songs. In contrast, Beatles' songs were filled with energy, a refreshing change from the slower songs. The words were bouncy and fresh. The sound was polished and fun.

But the Beatles' appeal went beyond music. For one thing, they were sex symbols. Teenage girls—and in some cases their older sisters and mothers—were especially attracted by their hair, their clothes, their good looks, and their fame. But they were also safe and friendly sex symbols—not hard-edged troublemakers like some early rock 'n' rollers. And their image as fun-loving kids made them popular with everyone, not just women.

While The Beatles appealed to people in all age groups, their main audience was teenagers. And the size of that audience was another reason for Beatlemania. After World War II, many soldiers returned home to the United States, England, and other countries and started families. Lots of babies were born in a population swell that came to be called the baby boom. The baby boom generation was just reaching its teen years when The Beatles became popular. So one reason the craziness was larger was simply because there were more people to be crazy.

When The Beatles became popular, many baby boomers identified with them. Teenagers saw and heard their own energy and enthusiasm in The Beatles and their music. They saw and heard their own attitudes in The Beatles' performances and songs, and they wanted Beatles records.

The media, especially television, also played an important role in Beatlemania. Had The Beatles come on the scene a decade earlier, most people wouldn't have been able to see them outside of a live performance. Few families owned televisions in the early 1950s, and program offerings were limited. But the Ed Sullivan broadcast carried The Beatles into millions of homes. Their performances were shared experiences for the whole nation. Everyone could talk about them the next day, since nearly everyone had seen them.

Finally, Beatlemania fed more Beatlemania. Stories about fans going crazy in one place told fans in other places how they should act. Being a fan meant you could just go crazy. And they did.

Security often removed fans who became overwhelmed by Beatlemania.

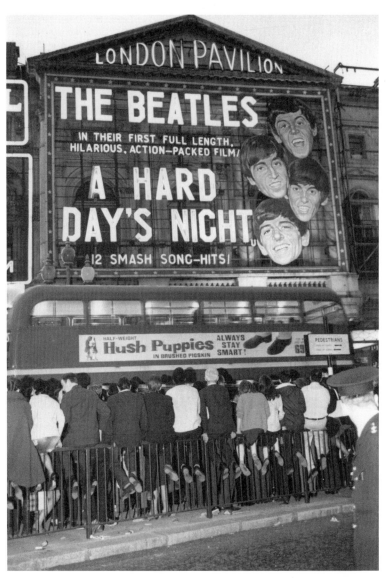

Large crowds formed outside the London Pavilion to see The Beatles' first feature film, which was released in 1964.

Chapter FOUR

A HARD DAY'S NIGHT

No ONE NOTICED THE OLD GENTLEMAN AS HE walked toward the crowd. They were too busy waiting for a glimpse of their heroes inside the television studio. The man tried to get their attention, but no one heard. Then he announced loudly that he had Beatles pictures—signed by the Fab Four themselves. In an instant, young girls surrounded him, clamoring for the photos. He could have sold a thousand if he'd had them. Then again, he was lucky he wasn't simply run over by the desperate fans.

This scene wasn't real—it's actually from a movie, *A Hard Day's Night,* which The Beatles began filming after returning from the United States in February 1964. But the scene and the movie neatly summed up

Beatlemania. The Beatles were in demand for everything and anything: concerts, albums, television shows, films, photos, dolls, mugs, toys, pennants, even lamps. Anything with their picture or simply their name on it sold. The world couldn't seem to get enough of them.

A Hard Day's Night made fun of Beatlemania. It featured a lot of Beatles' music and plenty of gags, sort of like a Marx Brothers or a Keystone Kops movie, with music videos thrown in. The plot is simplistic—the Beatles play themselves on their way to a television performance. Girls chase the band members down the streets. They're admitted everywhere and forgiven everything. The film captures the zaniness that surrounded John, Paul, George, and Ringo in real life. The movie also hints at some of the work behind the fame: the many rehearsals, the boredom of traveling, the temptations like drinking and gambling. Directed by Richard Lester, *A Hard Day's Night* was a big success when it was released in July 1964. So was its soundtrack album, which came out in August.

During the shooting of the film, George met Pattie Boyd, an actress with a minor role in the movie. They began dating and eventually married. At first, however, they kept their relationship as quiet as possible. Publicity about girlfriends would interfere with female fans' fantasies about dating and marrying one of The Beatles. More than their image as eligible bachelors was at stake, however. Jealous fans were constantly harassing The Beatles' girlfriends and John's wife, Cynthia. Privacy was becoming more and more important to the band members—and more and more difficult to maintain.

"Can't Buy Me Love"

The *Hard Day's Night* soundtrack included a song called "Can't Buy Me Love." Instantly a Beatles classic, the song reminds listeners that money isn't everything. That simple idea was an important one for The Beatles, who repeated it often. Many of their fans, young and idealistic, fervently agreed.

Not that The Beatles didn't care about money at all. It couldn't buy love, but it could buy a lot. And John,

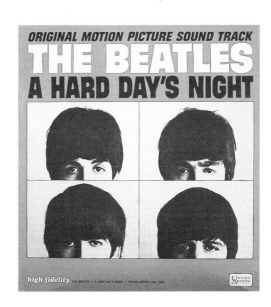

The album cover for A Hard Day's Night (1964) shows The Beatles' signature haircuts.

Paul, George, and Ringo suddenly had more money than they ever had before. John, for example, soon bought a Rolls-Royce, a Ferrari, and a Mini Cooper sports car.

Even so, The Beatles weren't rich. Before they were famous, they had agreed to perform concerts at relatively low rates. The record contract with Parlophone, signed when they were unknown, was also very stingy. And while companies were churning out everything from Beatles T-shirts to Beatles lamps, The Beatles themselves got very little payment from the use of their name.

Using a group's name and image on products this way is called merchandising. The practice is commonplace, but it was new for rock bands when The Beatles

Beatles merchandise included everything from figurines to board games featuring the Fab Four.

became famous. At first, the band members ended up with only a small percentage of the profits. Although they eventually made new agreements with higher fees, the small cut rankled The Beatles. They saw that others were getting rich off their hard work.

Another deal that hurt The Beatles severely had to do with the ownership of their songs. John Lennon and Paul McCartney composed most of the early Beatles songs. They made a deal with a small music publisher and formed a separate company called Northern Songs, which would own and publish all Lennon-McCartney songs. Unfortunately, the deal gave The Beatles and Brian Epstein only 49 percent of the company's shares. That meant they didn't control the company, and they didn't fully own or control their songs. The songs could be used in advertisements without their permission, for example. What's more, a lot of the company's profits went not to Paul and John but to other shareholders.

BACK TO THE USA

Before they were famous, The Beatles played as many gigs as they could. They did the same thing after they became famous, only for much larger audiences. In August 1964, they left England for a full tour of the United States. Starting in San Francisco, the band gave twenty-six shows in little more than a month.

At the Gator Bowl in Jacksonville, Florida, the promoter wanted black audience members separated from whites, a practice that was common in the American South at the time. The band refused to go on until their black fans were allowed to sit with the rest of the audience. To lure the band to play in Kansas City, a businessman named Charles Finley paid them $150,000 up front, about six times their normal rate. Even their normal rate of $25,000 per show was unheard of for performers at the time.

Hits like "Twist and Shout," "All My Loving," "She Loves You," "Can't Buy Me Love," "I Want to Hold Your Hand," "A Hard Day's Night," and Little Richard's "Long Tall Sally" were all standard parts of the shows on the American tour. So was nearly non-stop screaming by teenage girls, who sometimes threw and waved underwear at the group. At least twice, berserk fans interrupted concerts.

When they got back to England, the band began recording a new album and then started another British tour. While the places they played in were smaller than the American venues, the crowds were just as enthusiastic. Beatlemania was in full bloom.

Pushing the Limits

The songs in the standard Beatles shows were familiar to the fans. They were mostly hits as singles. They fit in the line of traditional rock 'n' roll that The Beatles had played since their early Liverpool days.

The Beatles had given rock their own spin and accent, but their sound was still heavily influenced by

AUDIO TECHNOLOGY

odern computers make it possible to "construct" a record from many separate tracks, or recordings. Engineers can record each instrument or voice separately and can then manipulate the tracks in many ways. They can speed up or slow down the music. They can stop it and restart it. They can slice bits of music away. They can also synthesize, or create, a wide variety of sounds from scratch. They can combine different tracks in endless ways.

But none of these techniques were possible when The Beatles began making records. Instead, the entire group had to play and sing at once, and the whole performance was taped. If one band member made a mistake—or if the engineer goofed—everybody had to start again.

The technology for playing back recorded music was also very basic during the early 1960s. Surround Sound and systems such as Dolby 5.1 were unheard of then. Most people listened to music on small radios or turntables. The equipment was monophonic, meaning that it played just one recorded track through a single speaker. Stereophonic equipment, which played music from two tracks through two speakers, was still new when The Beatles began recording.

earlier groups. In the recording studio, though, The Beatles' creativity took them in new directions. "She's a Woman," a song on the *Beatles for Sale* album, showed a strong blues influence. "Eight Days a Week," also on *Beatles for Sale*, began with a recording technique called a fade up, an unusual twist. On *Rubber Soul*, released in December 1965, "What Goes On" had a definite country-western feel. On the same album, "Nowhere Man" broke completely with usual pop song themes, telling the story of a man removed from normal life. The band's sound was evolving and expanding.

The Beatles took their musical experimentation even further with *Revolver*, released in 1966. One song on the album, "Eleanor Rigby," tells about a lonely old woman forgotten by society. In the future, other Beatles songs would address serious topics like peace and social justice. Other performers of the day, especially folk musicians like Bob Dylan, were also writing songs about such topics. But The Beatles showed that pop music, too, could make a political statement.

George Martin, who produced The Beatles' records from the beginning, played an important role in their evolution. He helped The Beatles arrange their music—figuring out the parts for each instrument and voice. As the producer, he also oversaw recording and engineering. He introduced techniques such as overdubbing, which involves using two tapes of the same vocal part to add depth to a recorded song. These techniques have since become standard in the music industry, but at the time they were innovations.

The willingness to innovate and experiment made The Beatles truly different from the bands that had come before. Not only were they wildly successful but they also continued to experiment. And their experiments were also wildly successful. Their popularity made it possible for them to try new creative techniques. Their musical abilities made the techniques they tried work.

BIGGER THAN GOD

During the summer of 1965, The Beatles were as popular as ever. Their songs dominated the pop charts throughout the world. When they arrived by helicopter in New York's Shea Stadium for a concert that summer, the screams of the crowd drowned out the roar of the helicopter's engines.

But fame had a dark side. Before and after performances, the band was mobbed and sometimes followed. When they weren't traveling or performing, John, Paul, George, and Ringo were often confined to their hotel rooms, prisoners of their own fame. Their image as lovable mop tops also felt like a straitjacket. They weren't supposed to do anything that conflicted with that image. The enormous media attention made misunderstandings inevitable.

In the summer of 1966, one misunderstanding caused a strong reaction against the group. In an interview with reporter Maureen Cleave, John Lennon talked about religion. He said that religion had become irrelevant for many teenagers. To illustrate his point, he casually mentioned that The Beatles were

In 1966 teenagers burned records in protest because of John Lennon's public comments about religion.

better known than Jesus Christ. Several months later, the quote was reprinted out of context. Reporters twisted it, implying that Lennon had said that The Beatles were more important than God.

Immediately, a number of right-wing groups, including southern churches and the Ku Klux Klan, attacked The Beatles. Radio stations, especially in "the Bible Belt" of the southern United States, made a show of burning Beatles records—even though some of the stations had never played the records to begin with. Even before Lennon's comment, the group had been an inviting target for criticism. They were well known and well liked. Attacking them was an easy way to get attention. They were also a symbol of teenagers, who seemed to be getting more rebellious as the sixties went on. Many adults blamed The Beatles for this new rebellious attitude. Lennon's remark only added to the hostility.

Maureen Cleave tried to correct the distortion, explaining that the quote was taken from a long conversation. "He observed that the power of Christianity was on the decline in the modern world and that things had reached such a ridiculous state that human beings—such as The Beatles—could be worshipped more religiously by people than their own religion," said Cleave. "He did not mean to boast about The Beatles' fame."

In August, John Lennon met with reporters to explain and apologize. "I never meant it as a lousy anti-religious thing," he said at a hostile press conference in Chicago. "I'm not anti-God, anti-Christ, or anti-religion. I was not saying we're greater or better. I believe in God but not as an old man in the sky. I believe what people call God is something in all of us. I wasn't saying The Beatles are better than God or Jesus."

THE END OF TOURING

The Jesus remark gained The Beatles a lot of negative attention. Suggesting that some Beatles concerts were not 100 percent full, reporters hinted that Beatlemania was over. But it was not. The band members were

still mobbed wherever they went. Record sales continued to be strong. Concerts fetched huge sums.

If anyone was looking for Beatlemania to end,
though, it was The Beatles themselves. The heavy
schedule of touring, as well as the manic crowds, took
a toll. Concerts especially frustrated the group. The

The Beatles rest after a live performance.

only places large enough to hold the vast numbers of fans they attracted were sports stadiums and large arenas. But the audio technology of the day guaranteed that the sound quality in such places would be terrible. And the howl from the crowd often made it impossible for The Beatles to hear themselves play.

Eventually, they stopped caring how they sounded. The group that had made its name with tight performances fell out of step. They didn't bother to rehearse. They were playing poorly and hated it. "It's got too far from the Cavern," said John.

Separately and then together, the band members came to the conclusion to stop touring. On August 29, 1966, the band rocked Candlestick Park in San Francisco. It was their last organized concert as a group. "Well that's it. I'm finished. I'm not a Beatle anymore," George reportedly said on the airplane home.

The Beatles might have been exhausted and disgusted by Beatlemania. But they were far from finished. Their best—and worst—was yet to come.

The Beatles' new wild style became apparent as they filmed Magical Mystery Tour.

Chapter **FIVE**

MAGICAL MYSTERY TOUR

THE TYPICAL AMERICAN HIGH SCHOOL YEARBOOK OF 1962 or 1963 shows young men with close-cropped haircuts and suits and ties. Young women appear in dresses and skirts that fall below their knees, their hair carefully set. In even the most casual photographs of this era, students seem extremely careful, even stilted, in their appearance. Their clothes seem very formal to our eyes.

Pick up a yearbook from five or six years later, and all the styles have changed. Many boys have hair below their ears and in some cases beyond their shoulders. Jeans are the most common item of clothing, worn by students of both sexes. Beads, medallions, wild colors, and casual clothes are the norm.

Fashions changed remarkably during the 1960s. The Beatles helped pave the way for some of these changes—long hair on boys, for example. But the dramatic changes in hair and fashion were only a small part of a whirlwind of change that shook society in the 1960s. Across the United States, young people challenged accepted ideas about sex, race, religion, careers, and women's roles in society. Longhaired "hippies" wore wild clothes and talked about peace and love. Many young people experimented with drugs. At speeches, marches, and demonstrations, many college students violently denounced U.S. involvement in the Vietnam War.

In many cases, the older generation resisted these changes. Discussions on a variety of topics—beginning with the length of boys' hair—pitted parents against teenagers in many households. Commentators called this division between young and old the "generation gap."

The Beatles were at the center of this youthful rebellion, and they quickly took up the new styles themselves. In the mid-1960s, they stopped wearing their formal suits and began wearing psychedelic clothing, decorated with wild colors and unusual patterns. They grew their hair even longer than before and grew mustaches and beards. They began to experiment with illegal drugs and Eastern religions. John Lennon became an outspoken advocate of peace.

Millions of young fans followed the band members' lead, experimenting with new ideas and new fashions.

Many young people rushed to buy wire-rimmed "granny glasses," just like those that John Lennon wore. The Beatles' popularity as rock stars made them extremely influential, even though they hadn't set out to be. In the few short years and many long, hard nights since their appearance on *The Ed Sullivan Show*, The Beatles had become role models for an entire generation.

On Top—and Beat

By late 1966, The Beatles were the most successful group in the history of pop music. Whether their achievements were measured in money, fame, or creative output, no one else came close. In four years, they recorded and released seven LPs in the United Kingdom: *Please Please Me* (1963), *With the Beatles* (1963), *A Hard Day's Night* (1964), *Beatles for Sale* (1964), *Help!* (1965), *Rubber Soul* (1965), and *Revolver* (1966). They had also put out a shorter record called *Long Tall Sally* (1964). Thirteen albums with mostly the same songs had been released in the United States. A dozen singles had gone to number one in England; another dozen had topped the charts in the United States. The Beatles had acted and played music in two movies, *A Hard Day's Night* (1964) and *Help!* (1965), a spoof of the James Bond films. They had played around the world to sellout crowds. More people knew who they were than could be counted.

But The Beatles were also tired, exhausted by their years of hard work. Since the late 1950s, John, Paul, and George had been constant companions. Beatlemania locked them together on a never-ending roller coaster. They careened from studios to limos to concert halls to airplanes to hotel rooms and back around again. When their 1966 American tour ended, they returned home and began their first long vacation away from each other.

George went to India with his wife, Pattie, to study Indian music. While there, they became interested in Indian spiritual beliefs. John joined the peace movement and took a supporting role in an antiwar film

John Lennon was an important figure in antiwar protests. Here he appears in the 1967 antiwar film, How I Won the War.

called *How I Won the War.* Living in London, Paul spent a lot of time with avant-garde artists who were exploring new concepts such as performance art. Ringo married his girlfriend, Maureen Cox, in February 1965. During the summer of 1966, they bought a house in London and fixed it up. Ringo spent much of his time with Maureen and their first son, Zak, born in September 1965.

GOING HOME IN SONG

In late November 1966, The Beatles got back together in the studio. They began recording a new song written by John, "Strawberry Fields Forever," inspired by a real place near John's childhood home. A Salvation Army camp, Strawberry Fields hosted flower shows each summer, and John tried to evoke the feeling of those shows in his song. His words and music are like a lighthearted walk through a summer garden. In the studio, John and the other Beatles made the song into a kind of "sound picture." They added orchestral music, sound effects such as cymbals recorded and played backward, and unusual instruments to more traditional vocal and musical styles.

Producer George Martin played an especially important role in recording this song. He helped "construct" the sound images. Even more important, he spliced together two completely different versions of the song. When Lennon suggested that George put the two takes together, Martin was dumbfounded. "They're in two different keys and they're also in different tempos," he protested.

"I'm sure you can fix it," Lennon told him. Then he walked away.

Martin did fix it. He changed the speed on both recordings, bringing the keys and the tempos together. He then spliced the songs seamlessly together. "If you want to know where the two songs are actually joined," Martin said later, "it's exactly one minute in from the beginning."

"Strawberry Fields Forever" was like no other rock 'n' roll song ever produced. It relied heavily on recording technology as well as creativity. It also required a producer like George Martin—a person who could pull the complicated strands together. And it was only the beginning.

A LEAP BEYOND

The music and sound of "Strawberry Fields Forever" were radical, but the song's subject was a return home for John—he was writing about Liverpool and his childhood. His songwriting was gradually becoming more autobiographical. More and more, he wrote directly from his own experiences and feelings.

Another song, written by Paul and recorded around the same time, was also a return to Liverpool. It was "Penny Lane," named after a street in the city. While Paul changed a few details, the words paint an accurate picture of the Penny Lane area. Both Beatles seemed to be nostalgic for simpler times, even as they raced ahead.

The group planned the songs for a new album. But their record company wanted The Beatles to release a single, knowing it would be a hit. So the two songs were put back-to-back on a 45, released in February 1967. Critics and other musicians immediately realized that The Beatles were going in a new and exciting direction.

The group continued working on songs for a new album, and they wanted it to have a common theme. They had first intended to build the album around the returning home theme of "Strawberry Fields Forever" and "Penny Lane," but that idea fell by the wayside. Then Paul began writing a song called "Sgt. Pepper's Lonely Hearts Club Band." The Beatles were off in a new direction and never looked back.

"Just an ordinary song, not particularly brilliant as songs go," said George Martin. "When we'd finished it, Paul said, 'Why don't we make the whole album as though the Pepper Band really existed, as though Sgt. Pepper was doing the record. We can dub effects and things.' From that moment, it was as if Pepper had a life of its own."

This idea gave the album, also called *Sgt. Pepper's Lonely Hearts Club Band,* a loose theme—it was supposed to contain songs performed by a pretend pop band. Careful listening shows that the lyrics and music of the different songs don't have much in common.

SIXTIES ROCK AND ROLL

I n the wake of The Beatles' fame, rock 'n' roll's popularity zoomed in the 1960s. As it did, fans' tastes changed. British groups such as the Dave Clark Five, the Animals, Gerry and the Pacemakers, Manfred Mann, and the Searchers followed The Beatles in the mid-1960s. These groups that featured upbeat melodies and Beatles-style harmonies. British bands that had a harder, guitar-driven beat—groups like the Rolling Stones, the Who, and the Kinks—emerged in the late 1960s.

American bands reflected the same changing tastes. The Doors, the Velvet Underground (featuring Lou Reed), Carlos Santana, Jefferson Airplane, the Grateful Dead, and Creedence Clearwater Revival took the stage as the 1960s continued, each adding their own contributions to rock 'n' roll. Performers like Jimi Hendrix and Janis Joplin, influenced by earlier blues musicians as well as rock, added unique instrumental and vocal styles to the genre.

Folk music, which had thrived in the early sixties, turned toward rock later in the decade. Showing the way was singer-songwriter Bob Dylan, a friend of the Beatles, who added a rock beat to many of his folksongs. Other American folk-rockers included the Byrds, the Lovin' Spoonful, the Mamas and the Papas, the Turtles, and Buffalo Springfield. They, too, felt the pull toward a harder, edgier sound as the decade went on.

Bob Dylan became well known for his political folksongs.

What they do share, however, is intense studio experimentation. Influenced by *Pet Sounds,* an album by the Beach Boys, The Beatles pushed recording technology to the limit to weave a sound tapestry. George Martin and the engineers used many audio tricks, like adding sound effects and slowing down or speeding up the tape to change the sound of a voice or instrument. The album went beyond anything done in pop music before, and its success led to more technological innovations.

LUCY IN THE SKY

One of the album's most famous songs was "Lucy in the Sky with Diamonds." The music starts slowly, then careens wildly. The lyrics seem fantastical. The strange sounds and lyrics and the initials of the main words in the title—LSD—seemed to refer to the mind-altering drug LSD. Many young people, including The Beatles, were experimenting with this drug at the time. Many listeners concluded that the song celebrated drugs and was based on a drug trip.

John actually began writing the song by describing a picture drawn by his young son, Julian. The picture, Paul explained, showed a girl floating in the sky with diamonds. "He played me the idea he had for it, starting with 'Picture yourself,'" Paul told George Martin later. "We discussed Lewis Carroll and the Alice [in Wonderland] books and how this title would make a great psychedelic song. We began to trade images

John with his son, Julian, in 1967 at their home in Weybridge, England

with each other. I suggested 'cellophane flowers.'. . . John countered with 'the girl with kaleidoscope eyes.'" Paul said the LSD connection was something they realized only later.

Other songs on the album included "A Day in the Life," "With a Little Help from My Friends," and "When I'm Sixty-Four." The album cost £25,000 to make—a huge sum for a rock album at the time and about twenty times what the first Beatles album had cost to produce. It took nearly five months to complete. It was The Beatles' riskiest and most expensive album ever.

It was an immediate smash.

An Unhappy Success

Brian Epstein had been critical to The Beatles' success. Besides managing The Beatles, he also managed other musical groups and ran a successful management company, NEMS. He owned a large portion of a London theater. With two homes and a great deal of wealth, he was by most definitions successful.

But he was also unhappy and under a great deal of stress. He may have been worried about his future with The Beatles, since his contract with them was due to run out in 1967. He was in no danger of being replaced, but if the group didn't tour, his role would be less important. At some point, Epstein began taking sleeping pills. He also drank heavily and occasionally used other drugs, including amphetamines. At times his drug use was out of control.

On the weekend of August 25, 1967, all four Beatles traveled by train to Bangor, Wales, to meet an Indian spiritual teacher named Maharishi Mahesh Yogi. He was teaching transcendental meditation, an Eastern meditation technique. George, who had visited India the year before, introduced Indian spiritual practices to the other Beatles. On the spur of the moment, they decided to visit the Maharishi and learn firsthand

After successfully managing The Beatles for years, the stress finally became too much for Brian Epstein.

about his beliefs. Several friends, including Mick Jagger of the Rolling Stones, traveled with them.

Brian Epstein was invited to join them over the weekend. He never showed. On Sunday afternoon, the band members got a call saying that Brian had been found dead in his London apartment. An investigation showed that he had died from an accidental overdose of sleeping pills.

A NEW PHASE

Shaken, The Beatles returned to London. *Sgt. Pepper* had shattered the early Beatles image as lovable mop tops. The album's music took them far beyond their rock roots. With Brian Epstein's death, they were about to enter a new phase in their business careers as well.

Before Brian Epstein's death, The Beatles had planned to create a new company to coordinate their business interests. With Epstein's death, this company became much more important, and the band members took a more direct role in it than previously planned. The company was called Apple Corps, or simply Apple. It would be the "core" of their operation, managing their record releases, films, and other creative projects. The company would have a record division to produce other artists' music. An Apple Boutique would sell clothes and other items. A division called Apple Films would release movies. "It's a business concerning records, films, and electronics and, as a sideline, manufacturing or whatever," explained John at a press conference announcing Apple. "We want to set up a system whereby people who just want to make a film about anything don't have to go on their knees in somebody's office [beg a producer]."

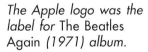

The Apple logo was the label for The Beatles Again *(1971) album.*

The Beatles wanted Apple to be less greedy and more democratic than other companies. They wanted the business to be fun, explained Peter Brown, a longtime Beatles associate and the company's administrative director. But managing the money and business details of the band was complicated. Individual Beatles had different ideas about how the company should operate, and these differences led to conflicts. The British government also took a high percentage of their income in taxes, which put further strain on the group.

As the band's manager, Brian Epstein had overseen all of their business arrangements. "When Brian Epstein was alive," explained Epstein's biographer, Ray Coleman, "nothing went wrong for The Beatles; when he died, little went right for them outside of music." Coleman explained that Brian had allowed The Beatles to do what they did best—make music. With Apple, the band members were soon in unfamiliar territory.

A FILM FLOP

In September 1967, The Beatles began filming a movie called *Magical Mystery Tour*. Conceived mostly by Paul, the film was supposed to represent a psychedelic trip—sort of the movie equivalent of the *Sgt. Pepper* music. The film showed The Beatles and friends boarding a bus and wandering around the countryside. Their fantasy experiences would be as important as the real places they visited.

The songs that were part of the film, including "Fool on the Hill" and "I Am the Walrus," continued the experiments and recording techniques used with *Sgt. Pepper.* Many of the songs quickly became classics. The film, however, was chaotic and uneven. Broadcast on British television around Christmas, it flopped.

Many people attacked the movie, claiming it advocated drug use. Others criticized its disjointed and experimental style. "If they were not The Beatles, the BBC [British Broadcasting Corporation] would not have fallen for it," said the *Daily Mirror.* "Beatles bomb with Yule [Christmastime] film," said the *Los Angeles Times.* The film was never shown in United States, even though the album quickly topped the charts.

Paul McCartney standing next to the tour bus from The Beatles' Magical Mystery Tour.

John met Yoko Ono, left, *at an art show in 1966.*

Chapter **SIX**

CRASH

JOHN **LENNON, BEMUSED AND A LITTLE CONFUSED,** climbed up a stepladder. Above his head was a piece of canvas. A small spyglass, or telescope, was suspended from a chain. When he reached the top of the ladder, Lennon put his eye to the spyglass. He maneuvered the glass toward the canvas, aligning it to read a message, a single word in capital letters: YES.

Yes.

Yes? Was it art? Or something else?

Yes.

Lennon was visiting an art show at the Indica Gallery in London. The ladder hadn't been left by a workman. It was part of a show prepared by Yoko Ono, an avant-garde American artist. The show featured odd items, including a bag of nails, and an apple with a £200 price tag.

"You're on this ladder," Lennon told an interviewer years later, "you feel like a fool, you could fall any minute—and you look through it and it just says 'YES.' Well, all the so-called avant-garde art at the time, and everything that was supposedly interesting, was all . . . boring, negative crap. It was all anti-, anti-, anti-. Anti-art, anti-establishment. And just that 'YES' made me stay in a gallery full of apples and nails instead of just walking out."

NEW LOVES

Seven years older than Lennon and married to her second husband, Yoko Ono seems to have fallen in love with John Lennon from the moment they were introduced at the show in late 1966. John had been married to Cynthia Powell for several years, but Yoko sent him cryptic notes and managed to stay in touch. Although John had lost interest in his marriage, he wasn't attracted to Yoko at first. He did, however, provide funding for another exhibit of Yoko's work. And he gradually grew more interested in her as well as her art.

In May 1968, while his wife was away in Greece, John invited Yoko to come listen to some avant-garde music he was creating in his basement studio. When Cynthia returned from her vacation, she found Yoko and John in their bathrobes having breakfast. Within a few weeks, the Beatle and the waiflike avant-garde artist would be inseparable.

Paul McCartney's love life also changed around this time. In May 1967, at a press reception for *Sgt. Pepper* in London, he met a young American photographer named Linda Eastman. A divorced mother, Linda had recently made a name for herself photographing rock stars. She was tall, intelligent, and good-looking, with long blond hair and a self-assured manner. Her father was a well-known attorney in New York City, with many clients in the entertainment industry. The following year, Paul and Linda ran into each other again in the United States. Soon they began dating. The relationship flourished, and they later married.

THE WHITE ALBUM

The Beatles' search for spiritual guidance took them to India in early 1968, again to study with the Maharishi Mahesh Yogi. Ringo left India after two weeks, when he and his wife got homesick, but the others stayed and studied meditation and other spiritual practices. They also continued to write songs, finishing forty while they were there. "It was really very interesting and I will continue to meditate," Paul said when he decided to leave India after five weeks. John and George stayed on for two more weeks, but they began to grow disenchanted with their spiritual teacher. John especially began to doubt that the Maharishi had any real answers about life. Finally, after rumors that the religious leader was having an affair with one of the other students, John and George left too.

John's song "Sexy Sady" is a barely disguised denouncement of the Maharishi. The song was part of a two-record album that The Beatles began recording in the summer of 1968. The album once again broke new ground—in part because of its music but more because it featured The Beatles as individual musicians rather than a group. The band members worked more

The Beatles studied with the Maharishi Mahesh Yogi, center, *for many years before they began to doubt the Yogi's wisdom.*

independently on songs than ever before. John, Paul, and George each created some tracks almost single-handedly, with little help from the others.

Although it was officially called *The Beatles*, fans called the records the White Album because the cover was pure white, with only the words "The Beatles" printed on the front. It was the first two-record set for the group. The album showed off the wide range of The Beatles' songwriting interests. Like those on *Sgt. Pepper* and *Magical Mystery Tour*, the tracks were constructed with overdubs, sound effects, and various instruments. But the album also contained straight-forward rockers that updated the group's early sound.

Among these songs was "Back in the USSR." Written by Paul in India, the song is a takeoff of an early Chuck Berry tune ("Back in the USA"). The song also contains a tribute to and parody of the Beach Boys. Mostly known for their surfing songs and tight harmonies, the group had always been considered a serious competitor to The Beatles. In this track, The Beatles showed they could master the California surf sound that the Beach Boys had popularized.

"Revolution 1," written by John, has The Beatles on heavy guitar riffs. The words express John's political philosophy, encouraging peaceful change to make the world better. Paul's "Ob-la-di, Ob-la-da" features a play-ful, easygoing rhythm. So does John's "The Continuing Story of Bungalow Bill," but its lyrics are more complex. In this song, Lennon uses irony to put forth an antigun and antihunter message. George Harrison wrote several songs for the album, including one of his best-known compositions, "While My Guitar Gently Weeps." The song featured the guitar playing of George's friend Eric Clapton, who was becoming a rock icon in his own right when the recording was made.

The most controversial song on the album is "Revolution 9," which is more of a sound collage than a song. It contains orchestral music, seemingly random voices, and bits of jumbled sound effects that all seem to run together in a sometimes melodic, sometimes maddening flow. The piece has a definite movement, but it doesn't sound like a traditional rock or pop song.

CONFLICT

George Martin felt that some of the material on the *White Album* should have been left out. He felt that a single album would have been stronger than a double one. On the other hand, releasing a double album let The Beatles express a wide range of musical styles. It may also have helped them avoid arguments about whose material to use. For the first time in their history, differences in personalities and musical interests were causing serious creative conflicts.

At first, the differences seemed petty, at least when viewed from a distance. John was upset because Paul didn't ask him to work on a song he liked. The others called Paul too much of a perfectionist. At one point, Ringo quit the sessions, saying he was leaving the

*John's love interest, Yoko Ono, often sat in on The Beatles'
rehearsals, much to the irritation of the other band members.*

band. But he returned after two weeks.

Yoko Ono was another source of irritation. During
the recording for *The White Album,* she sat in on the
sessions. She perched on the band's monitor speakers,
which irked Paul. She also whispered to John and
offered advice to the others, which they clearly did not
want. From Paul's point of view, she was an interfering
know-it-all, out for John's money and fame. And she
knew nothing about rock 'n' roll, the other Beatles
said. Eventually, everything she did bothered someone.

Yoko had become a kind of muse, or inspiration, to
John, but there were other reasons he wanted her close
to him that summer. Yoko was pregnant, and he was
concerned about her health. (She suffered a miscarriage
in November 1968.) Above all, John's relationship with
Yoko was a deep one, far more important to him than

his marriage to Cynthia. "I'm JOHNANDYOKO" he would write and say many times.

John resented the group's attitude toward Yoko. He and Yoko soon divorced their spouses and married one another in Gibraltar, an island near Spain, in 1969. John's song "The Ballad of John and Yoko" recounts the wedding.

One bright spot for the Beatles in 1968 was the release of a third Beatles movie, *Yellow Submarine*. A full-length animated feature, it instantly became a hit. Directed by George Dunning, the movie has a light plot inspired by The Beatles' song of the same name, part of the 1966 *Revolver* album. In the movie, cartoon Beatles battle the Blue Meanies, making the seas safe for civilization—or at least rock 'n' roll.

The band members actually had little to do with the project. Other actors provided the voices for their cartoon characters, and the band recorded only a few songs for the movie. The soundtrack album included an entire side of instrumentals arranged by George Martin. The music did not match the standards of The Beatles' other albums. Even so, the movie was well received and helped boost The Beatles' popularity.

But not much else was going right for The Beatles. Their friendships were clearly strained, and the situation soon got much worse. Apple Corps, the company set up to manage the band's business affairs, was supposed to be as revolutionary as the Beatles' music. But it quickly became a mess. The Apple

Boutique was perhaps the worst example. It opened on December 7, 1967, in a renovated building on Baker Street in London. The renovation itself had been chaotic, with the different Beatles ordering different construction work on whim. Once the store opened, the situation quickly turned sour. Shoplifting was rampant. "Garments began rapidly to leave the premises, though seldom as a result of cash transactions," writes Beatles biographer Philip Norman. The losses were immense. Finally, on July 30, 1968, the boutique ended its chaotic existence by giving away all of its merchandise.

Apple Corps continued on, however. The part of the company that made records had several successes with performers besides The Beatles, including singer James Taylor, but for the most part the business was out of control. Employees took advantage of free alcohol and practically nonstop parties—all funded by The Beatles. Hippies and Hells Angels (members of a rough motorcycle gang) roamed the halls. When the band members set up the company, they had each agreed to give all of their earnings to the business for ten years. "If Apple goes on at this rate," John told a journalist in 1969, "we'll be broke in six months." He calculated the losses at £20,000 a week. In modern U.S. money, that figure would amount to millions of dollars a year.

The Beatles surprise the London public with a free concert from the rooftop of Apple headquarters in 1969.

Chapter **SEVEN**

THE END OF
THE ROAD

ON JANUARY 30, 1969, THE COLD LONDON AIR
began jangling with something no fan had heard for
nearly three years: The Beatles together, live, whipping
through the chords of a fresh composition. With Paul
in sneakers and John wearing a woman's mink coat,
the group "made show" in central London. On a
makeshift stage atop the Apple headquarters building,
they tried out songs intended for a new album. For
the next forty minutes or so, the lunchtime crowd received a free, traffic-stopping rehearsal and concert.

The session began and ended with "Get Back," a
song that seemed to symbolize the entire project. The
hard-driving beat harkened back to The Beatles' earli-
est roots. The planned album, and a film that would

accompany it, were supposed to take The Beatles back to the spirit of their Hamburg days. The songs would be recorded live and would be released that way, mistakes and all. There would be no overdubbing. If John's fingers were too cold to play the chords right—as he complained following one song—that was just the way it was.

The London police brought the rooftop session to a premature end. It was a symbolic end to the Get Back project as well, though The Beatles struggled on for a few more sessions.

"THE LOW OF ALL TIME"

Because the Get Back project included a movie, much of the recording sessions were captured on film. The film shows a great deal of creativity on the part of band members, but almost as much bickering and bad feelings. The band members couldn't decide how the songs should be played. At different times, they wondered if they should bother with the project at all. "It was the low of all time," said George Harrison later. "The most miserable sessions on earth," noted John. At one point, the two friends traded angry punches. The project was soon scrapped.

Part of the problem had to do with being rusty. The Beatles prided themselves on polished performances and tight shows. But they hadn't performed as a complete band in a long time. They had learned to work independently in the studio and had lost the feel for one another. Even when they tried to pull off an update of "Love Me Do," they couldn't get it together.

As Beatles chronicler Mark Lewisohn wrote, "Although the Get Back project was supposed to be capturing The Beatles' rough edges, this recording was just too rough to be released." Two songs—"Get Back" and "Don't Let Me Down"—were culled for a single. The rest of the sessions remained on tape. Finally, more than a year later, they were heavily edited, remixed, and released as the album *Let It Be*.

The cause of The Beatles' problems in 1968 and 1969 was a combination of old and new strains. Apple and the chaos that surrounded it put incredible pressure on them. Paul and the others clashed over whom to hire to run the firm. Northern Songs, the company John and Paul originally formed to publish their music, slipped completely out of their control in a complicated series of business maneuvers. Not owning the songs they wrote was galling and frustrating. In the past, Brian Epstein had buffered the band members from business pressures and problems. He had also acted as peacemaker. Without him, the pull toward individual interests was much stronger.

The Beatles' use of drugs was also a strain. John used LSD, heroin, and other drugs during the late 1960s. As a result, his actions at times were erratic. He was arrested in 1968 for possession of marijuana. He eventually pleaded guilty to the charge and received a small fine. George Harrison was also arrested for drug possession after a raid on his home in Esher, England. Both George and his wife pleaded guilty to possession and were fined as well.

Most of all, creativity worked to push The Beatles apart. While remaining as prolific as ever, the band members were growing in different directions. They wanted to explore new music and new interests—but not all of these interests were shared by the others. Record albums could hold only a limited number of songs, so band members had to compromise. Collaborating had helped spark their creative genius. But it also constrained them.

George Harrison, who was blossoming as a songwriter, felt especially held back. He complained that he had written many songs worth recording that the others wouldn't even consider. In some ways, John and Paul treated him like a younger brother, not quite ready to play with the big boys. But that was nothing compared to how they treated each other. Their sessions were marked by bitterness and frustration. John had no patience for Paul's songs and music. Paul thought John was steering too far from melody. One of the greatest songwriting teams in the history of music now rarely agreed on anything.

The experience of playing and struggling together in the early days had welded The Beatles together. The bond was about more than just music. They were friends. As the disputes boiled over, the friendship at the center of The Beatles disintegrated. When it was gone, all that was left were four very talented individuals.

ABBEY ROAD

The Get Back project had been a disaster. The idea of playing live wouldn't work—The Beatles were not a live band anymore. But they were still The Beatles, and they still had plenty of songs they wanted to record. So they went to work on another batch. They worked separately on many of the tracks, much as they had on the White Album. The result was *Abbey Road,* which many critics rank as The Beatles' greatest album. It contained many songs that became instant classics.

George Harrison's "Something," for example, may be one of the best-loved songs of all time. "Come Together," written by John Lennon, is a hard-edged rocker that incorporates experimental sounds into a pop anthem. Paul McCartney seemed to go back to his fifties rock roots with "Oh! Darling." John and George influenced a generation or two of heavy metal rockers with the overlaid guitars on "I Want You (She's So Heavy!)."

The Beatles strode across this section of London's Abbey Road for the cover of their 1969 album. Abbey Road is still a popular place for Beatles fans to visit.

George Martin pointed out that the album's two sides have two different sounds. The first side is more stripped-down rock 'n' roll—the sound John wanted. "He wanted to get back to what he called 'honesty' in recording," said Martin. On the second side, the songs blend together like a symphonic suite—Paul's preference. John and Paul worked on songs on both sides of the album, but they were clearly going in different creative directions.

The album was a great success, but the band members felt that something was missing. Friction between them had hurt not just the group but also the record, Paul said. "On *Abbey Road* we don't do harmonies like we used to," he commented. "I think it's sad. On 'Come Together' I would have liked to sing harmony with John and I think he would have liked me to but I was too embarrassed to ask him." In short, The Beatles would never "come together" as The Beatles again.

In September John accepted an invitation to appear at a rock revival show in Canada. While he and Yoko had already performed in public without The Beatles, their music was experimental. The Toronto show was rock, and it was the first time a Beatle had performed at a major concert without The Beatles. After wailing through the numbers, Lennon came to the conclusion that had been inevitable for quite some time—The Beatles were over. "I might as well tell you, I'm leaving the group. I've had enough. I want a divorce, like my divorce from Cynthia," he told the others after he got back.

Paul wanted the group to continue. He kept pressing for a Beatles' live performance. George complained bitterly that the other two hadn't included his songs on their recent albums. The three longtime friends blew up at each other. As far as John was concerned, The Beatles had ceased to exist as a working band. But for business reasons, he agreed to keep his decision to leave the group quiet. No one spoke publicly about the breakup. To the outside world at least, The Beatles were still The Beatles.

It was Paul, not John, who made the break official. He retreated to his Scottish farm in the winter of 1969–1970. He and his wife, Linda, laid down the tracks for a solo album there. It was a true solo album, since Paul played all the instruments. Still, he seems to have hoped the group would remain together. But while he was working on his songs, Paul received a preview of *Let It Be,* the album created from the Get Back project. He was stunned. His song "The Long and Winding Road" had been meant as a simple ballad. He had recorded it that way. But the Beatles' new producer, Phil Spector, added violins, horns, and a choir to the final version. Furious, McCartney demanded that his version be restored, but it was not.

Paul McCartney had lost creative control of his music. The end of The Beatles had truly come.

John and Yoko often greeted fans at the entrance to the Dakota Hotel in New York City, where they lived.

Chapter **EIGHT**

AFTERLIFE

IT WAS WARM FOR DECEMBER. JOHN LENNON AND Yoko Ono told the limo driver to stop outside of the arched entrance to the Dakota Hotel, where they had their apartment in New York City. They liked to walk the last few steps to the building. Sometimes a few fans waited between the gate and the building to greet Lennon, but Beatlemania was long gone. It was 1980, and the Beatles had long since broken up. John Lennon was still famous, but he could usually walk around New York without being hounded or hassled.

John and Yoko were returning from a studio session that day, December 8. John carried the tapes from the session with him. They held a good piece of work—a song by Yoko for a new album. The couple had collaborated on a number of albums, and their latest one, *Double Fantasy,* had just come out. Critics said it was one of the best albums Lennon had ever worked on. Observers also noted that he seemed to have found a new peace to go along with his creative energy and ability.

Perhaps he had. In the decade since The Beatles had split up, John Lennon had passed through tumultuous times. First he kicked a severe drug habit and a drinking problem. Then he split with Yoko only to return to her, their love stronger than ever. They had a son, Sean, and John devoted himself to raising him. For a while, he called himself a "house husband." It was unusual at the time for a man to serve as an infant's primary caregiver, but John had a nurturing side—the opposite of the brash-talking rebel.

Of course, he hadn't given up making music. An early post-Beatles song, "Imagine," became as well known as anything he'd done with the band. He also played with hundreds of different musicians over the decade. Indeed, he had finally found peace after many hectic years.

John got out of the car and began striding through the gate toward the Dakota's front steps.

"Mr. Lennon?" shouted a man.

John Lennon turned around to see who was calling him. As he did, the man pumped five bullets into his back and arm.

Crowds gather outside the Dakota to express their shock and sadness after John Lennon's death.

Mortally wounded, Lennon stumbled into the Dakota. "I'm shot, I'm shot," he told the man at the front desk as he fell to floor. Within hours, he was dead.

Lennon's killer was a mentally disturbed man named Mark David Chapman. Chapman's sickness had apparently convinced him that *he* was the real John Lennon. He was found guilty of murder and sentenced to twenty years to life in prison.

THE FAB FOUR LIVE ON

John Lennon's death shocked the world and saddened millions of fans. And it seemed like there were as many Beatles fans as ever. By then, a new generation of young people loved The Beatles. Even after their

breakup, new records were released, including two dou-
ble-album greatest hits collections and a host of "best"
collections, live albums, and lesser-known recordings.
Bootlegs (illegal recordings) and books about The
Beatles appeared. Even in 2001, more than thirty years
after the breakup, Beatle memorabilia remained one of
the hottest items on Internet auction sites.

All of The Beatles had successful solo careers in the
decade following the band's demise. Paul McCartney,
with and without his new band, Wings, continued to be
a force in pop music. He made dozens of albums, including *McCartney*, his first solo effort, and *Wings over
America*, released in 1976. George Harrison's *All Things
Must Pass* was released to critical acclaim in 1970. His
Concert for Bangladesh, a live event recorded as a two-
album set in 1971, brought some of the world's best
rock musicians together to raise money for Bangladesh,
a small country ravaged by civil war and natural disas-
ters. Ringo Starr turned out several albums, recording
a top-ten hit with "You're Sixteen" in 1975.

The Beatles breakup did not end their financial
problems, though. At one point, Paul sued the group
in an attempt to dismantle the Beatles' partnership.
The dispute involved management of Apple, control of
The Beatles' business interests, and tax issues. The
legal battle brought new headaches and conflicts, but
tempers gradually "mellowed." Animosities and anger
died down, especially after John died. The surviving
members of the group continued to see each other

George Harrison at his charity concert for Bangladesh

and occasionally collaborated on projects. One of these collaborations involved finishing a song started by John before his death.

All the Beatles have been active in charities and other important causes. Before his death, John Lennon often helped groups devoted to peace. Yoko Ono continued that tradition. Paul McCartney has been active in a number of causes, including the fight against breast cancer, a disease that claimed the life of his wife, Linda, in 1999.

For all their individual success, none of the band members' solo albums or songs have the same impact as those they made as a group. The reasons are many. The Beatles came of age at a very special time. Changes in technology and society, along with the arrival of the baby boom generation, helped set the stage for them. As The Beatles, they created music that was about their time but would last beyond their time.

The group combined the genius and talents of the individual members, as well as the skills of others like George Martin. George Harrison's sweet guitar and Ringo Starr's steady beat were every bit as important as the lead singers' harmonies. The tension between John and Paul's different approaches was a necessary part of their success as songwriters. Ringo gave the others important advice on what worked or didn't work musically. The collaboration of different attitudes and experiences produced unique music. In this case, the old cliché "the sum is greater than the parts" was true.

It was not always a smooth relationship, but even with the bad feelings that surrounded the band's breakup, some part of the complicated friendship managed to survive. In his book, *Beatles Album,* Geoffrey Giuliano tells a story about John Lennon. A young woman saw him one day in New York City in the 1970s. He was wearing a vintage "I Love Paul" button from the days of Beatlemania. At the time, many newspaper stories said that John Lennon and Paul McCartney hated each other. So the woman asked John why he was wearing the button. "Because I love Paul," he told her.

Love fades, but somehow survives. And so does The Beatles music.

Many fans still remember what life was like in The Beatles' heyday. Like this 1965 concert in Shea Stadium, Queens, New York, every concert was sold out.

SOURCES

13 Hunter Davies, *The Beatles* (New York: W. W. Norton & Co., 1996), 21.

15 Ibid., 20.

17 Barry Miles, *Paul McCartney—Many Years from Now* (New York: Henry Holt and Company, 1997), 52.

18 Davies, *The Beatles*, 70.

20–21 David Pritchard and Alan Lysaght, *The Beatles, an Oral History* (New York: Hyperion, 1998), 41.

21 Bob Cepican and Ali Waleed, *Yesterday Came Suddenly* (New York: Arbor House, 1985), 71–72.

22 Miles, *Paul McCartney*, 74.

22 David Sheff, *The Playboy Interviews with John Lennon and Yoko Ono* (New York: Playboy Press, 1981), 142.

26 Brian Epstein, *A Cellarful of Noise* (New York: Pocketbooks, 1998), 105.

28 Ray Coleman, *The Man Who Made The Beatles—An Intimate Biography of Brian Epstein* (New York: McGraw-Hill, 1989), 97–98.

29 Davies, *The Beatles*, 135.

32 Ibid., 151.

32 Ray Coleman, *Lennon—The Definitive Biography* (New York: Harper Perennial, 1992), 264.

33 Davies, *The Beatles*, 163.

34 Sheff, *The Playboy Interviews*, 116.

34 Ross Benson, *Paul McCartney—Beyond the Myth* (London: Victor Gollanez, 1992), 178.

34 George Martin, *With A Little Help from My Friends—The Making of Sgt. Pepper* (New York: Little Brown and Company, 1994), 98.

35 Davies, *The Beatles*, 164.

38 Pritchard and Lysaght, *The Beatles, an Oral History*, 118.

38 Philip Norman, *Shout! The Beatles in Their Generation* (New York: Simon & Schuster, 1981), 177.

40 *The Complete Beatles*, dir. P. Montgomery and Stephanie Bennett (Teleculture, 1982), videocassette.

41   Gareth L. Pawlowski, *How They Became The Beatles* (New York: E. P. Dutton, 1989), 130.
41–42   Davies, *The Beatles*, 184.
44   Cepican and Ali, *Yesterday Came Suddenly*, 148.
45   Davies, *The Beatles*, 196.
59   Geoffrey Giuliano and Brenda Giuliano, *The Lost Beatles Interviews* (New York: Dutton, 1994), 69.
59   Cepican and Waleed, *Yesterday Came Suddenly*, 201.
59   Coleman, *Lennon*, 408.
61   Ibid., 410–411.
61   Cepican and Waleed, *Yesterday Came Suddenly*, 203.
68   David Pritchard and Alan Lysaght, *The Beatles, an Oral History*, 233–234.
69   Norman, *Shout!* 288.
71–72   Martin, *With a Little Help from My Friends*, 104.
75   Pritchard and Lysaght, *The Beatles, an Oral History*, 109.
76   Coleman, *The Man Who Made The Beatles*, 382.
77   Miles, *Paul McCartney*, 368.
77   Norman, *Shout!* 317.
80   Richard Buskin, *John Lennon, His Life and Legend* (Lincolnwood, IL: Publications International, 1991), 152. Quoting David Sheff, *The Playboy Interviews*, 1981.
81   Miles, *Paul McCartney*, 427.
86   Coleman, *Lennon*, 488.
87   Norman, *Shout!* 320.
87   Ibid., 360.
90   Mark Lewisohn, *The Complete Beatles Chronicle*, (London: Pyramid Books, 1992), 310.
90   Ibid.
91   Ibid., 311.
94   Martin, *With a Little Help from My Friends*, 139.
94   Miles, *Paul McCartney*, 552.
94–95   Norman, *Shout!* 385.
99   Coleman, *Lennon*, 679.
103   Geoffrey Giuliano, *The Beatles Album* (New York: Viking Studio Books, 1991), 218.

SELECTED BIBLIOGRAPHY

Bacon, David, and Norman Maslov. *The Beatles England.* San Francisco: 910 Press, 1982.

Benson, Ross. *Paul McCartney—Beyond the Myth.* London: Victor Gollancz, 1992.

Brown, Peter, and Steven Gaines. *The Love You Make.* New York: McGraw-Hill, 1983.

Cepican, Bob, and Ali Waleed. *Yesterday Came Suddenly.* New York: Arbor House, 1985.

Clayson, Alan. *Ringo Starr—Straight Man or Joker?* New York: Paragon House, 1992.

Coleman, Ray. *Lennon—The Definitive Biography.* New York: HarperCollins, 1992.

Davies, Hunter. *The Beatles.* New York: W. W. Norton & Company, 1996.

Epstein, Brian. *A Cellarful of Noise.* New York: Pocketbooks, 1998.

Giuliano, Geoffrey. *The Beatles Album.* New York: Viking Studio Book, 1991.

Giuliano, Geoffrey, and Brenda Giuliano. *The Lost Beatles Interviews.* New York: Dutton, 1994.

Harrison, George. *I, Me, Mine.* New York: Simon and Schuster, 1980.

Lewisohn, Mark. *The Complete Beatles Chronicle.* London: Pyramid Books, 1992.

Miles, Barry. *Paul McCartney—Many Years from Now.* New York: Henry Holt and Company, 1997.

Neises, Charles P., ed. *The Beatles Reader.* Ann Arbor, MI: Pierian Press, 1984.

Norman, Philip. *Shout! The Beatles in Their Generation.* New York: Simon and Schuster, 1981.

Pawlowski, Gareth L. *How They Became The Beatles.* New York: E. P. Dutton, 1989.

Pritchard, David, and Alan Lysaght. *The Beatles, an Oral History.* New York: Hyperion, 1998.

AN INTRODUCTORY DISCOGRAPHY

BRITISH RELEASES

Please Please Me, Parlophone Records, 1963
With the Beatles, Parlophone Records, 1963
A Hard Day's Night, Parlophone Records, 1964
Beatles for Sale, Parlophone Records, 1964
Help!, Parlophone Records, 1965
Rubber Soul, Parlophone Records, 1965
Revolver, Parlophone Records, 1966
A Collection of Beatles' Oldies, Parlophone Records, 1966
Sgt. Pepper's Lonely Hearts Club Band, Parlophone Records, 1967
The Beatles, Apple Records, 1968
Yellow Submarine, Apple Records, 1969
Abbey Road, Apple Records, 1969
Let It Be, Apple Records, 1970
The Beatles 1962–1966, Apple Records, 1973
The Beatles 1967–1970, Apple Records, 1973
The Beatles Live! At the Star Club in Hamburg, Germany: 1962,
    Lingasong, 1977
The Beatles at the Hollywood Bowl, Parlophone Records, 1977
Past Masters, Volumes One and Two, Apple Corps/EMI, 1988
The Beatles Anthology, Volumes 1, 2, and 3, Apple Corps/EMI,
    1995, 1996

U.S. RELEASES

Introducing the Beatles, Vee Jay Records, 1963
Meet the Beatles!, Capitol Records, 1964
The Beatles' Second Album, Capitol Records, 1964
A Hard Day's Night, United Artists Records, 1964
Something New, Capitol Records, 1964
The Beatles' Story, Capitol Records, 1964 (a documentary
    soundtrack with interviews)

Beatles '65, Capitol Records, 1964
The Early Beatles, Capitol Records, 1965 (contains many songs
    from the British *Please Please Me* album)
Beatles VI, Capitol Records, 1965
Help!, Capitol Records, 1965
Rubber Soul, Capitol Records, 1965
Yesterday and Today, Capitol Records, 1966
Revolver, Capitol Records, 1966
Sgt. Pepper's Lonely Hearts Club Band, Capitol Records, 1967
Magical Mystery Tour, Capitol Records, 1967
The Beatles, Apple Records, 1968
Yellow Submarine, Apple Records, 1969
Abbey Road, Apple Records, 1969
Let It Be, Apple Records, 1970
The Beatles 1962–1966, Apple Records, 1973
The Beatles 1967–1970, Apple Records, 1973
The Beatles Live! At the Star Club in Hamburg, Germany: 1962,
    Lingasong, 1977
The Beatles at the Hollywood Bowl, Parlophone Records, 1977
Past Masters Volumes One and Two, Apple Corps/EMI, 1988
The Beatles Anthology, Volumes 1, 2, and 3, Apple Corps/EMI,
    1995, 1996
The Beatles 1, Emd/Capitol, 2000

FILMOGRAPHY

FILMS FEATURING THE BEATLES
(ALL ARE CURRENTLY AVAILABLE ON VIDEO)

A Hard Day's Night, directed by Richard Lester, United Artists, 1964.
Help!, directed by Richard Lester, United Artists, 1965.
Magical Mystery Tour, directed by Dennis O'Dell, Apple Films, 1968.
Yellow Submarine, directed by George Dunning, MGA/UA, 1968.

DOCUMENTARIES ON THE BEATLES

The Compleat Beatles, directed by P. Montgomery and Stephanie
    Bennett, Teleculture, 1982.

Get Back, directed by Jordan Croneweth and Robert Paynter, Vestron Video, 1991.

The Beatles Anthology, directed by Geoff Wohfor, Capitol Video, 1996.

INDEX

OTHER TITLES FROM LERNER AND A&E®:

Arthur Ashe
Benjamin Franklin
Bill Gates
Bruce Lee
Carl Sagan
Chief Crazy Horse
Christopher Reeve
Edgar Allan Poe
Eleanor Roosevelt
George W. Bush
George Lucas
Gloria Estefan
Jack London
Jacques Cousteau
Jane Austen
Jesse Owens
Jesse Ventura
Jimi Hendrix
John Glenn
Latin Sensations
Legends of Dracula

Legends of Santa Claus
Louisa May Alcott
Madeleine Albright
Malcolm X
Mark Twain
Maya Angelou
Mohandas Gandhi
Mother Teresa
Nelson Mandela
Oprah Winfrey
Princess Diana
Queen Cleopatra
Queen Latifah
Rosie O'Donnell
Saint Joan of Arc
Thurgood Marshall
William Shakespeare
Wilma Rudolph
Women in Space
Women of the Wild West

ABOUT THE AUTHOR

Jeremy Roberts is the pen name of Jim DeFelice. He often uses this name when he writes for young readers, which he tries to do as much as he can. Besides this book, his recent nonfiction books include works on skydiving and rock climbing. He has written several installments in the Eerie, Indiana series and quite a few horror tales. His adult books include a historical trilogy and techno-thrillers. He lives with his wife and son in a haunted farmhouse in upstate New York.

PHOTO ACKNOWLEDGMENTS

Photographs used with permission of: Supplied by LA Media/ Retna, UK pp. 31; © Terrence Spencer/ Camera Press/Retna, Ltd. pp. 2; Hulton|Archive by Getty Images, pp. 6, 8, 16, 19, 36, 40, 48, 62, 72, 75, 77, 82, 88, 103; Photofest, pp. 10, 24, 29, 51, 52, 66, 85, 101; Globe Photos, Inc. pp. 15, 17, 20, 33, 44, 47, 60, 70, 74, 78, 96, 99; © Bettmann/CORBIS, pp. 28, 58; © Inge Yspeert/CORBIS, p. 93.

Hardcover: front, Globe Photos, Inc.; back, Hulton|Archive by Getty Images
Softcover: front, Globe Photos, Inc.; back, Globe Photos, Inc.